The Anointing of the Queen

SANDRA ALLEN

Unless otherwise indicated, all Scripture quotations are taken from the King James Version of the Bible.

The Anointing of the Queen

Dedicated to my Lord and Savior Jesus Christ

Preface

I thank the Lord for His goodness in my life. I give Him all the glory for being my God, my Comforter, and my friend.

What a glorious thing it is to be friends with God! When you understand the depth of His love for you, you can't help but draw close to Him. When you draw close to Him, He draws close to you and a wonderful relationship ensues. When you become close to the Lord, a trust develops and a confidence builds that underscores all that you do.

You trust that if God brings you to a place, He will not leave you. If He asks you to do something, He will equip you. As your relationship builds, you will come to the knowledge that you simply cannot fail in God. He will not allow it if you trust His Word and obey Him.

I hope that you come to know the Lord in a greater way after reading this book. I pray that you will love the Lord and be close enough to laugh, cry, and be silly with Him in your secret place.

What is the secret place? It is the place where you spend time alone with God to hear from Him, to feel His Presence, and to speak to Him. It is a place for just you and God. It is a place of visitation and love, but most of all, it is where God waits for you. He is your friend, your confidant, your advocate, and your greatest cheerleader.

My prayer for you is that as you read this book and embrace the greatness within, you will come to know the still, small voice of God, that sweet Fragrance that will make you laugh and Whose confidence in you will cause you to soar into your destiny.

My God, my friend.

Be Blessed,
Sandra Allen

Table of Contents

Introduction

What is the anointing? It is the power of God that enables us to do what we have been called to do and what He says we can become.

In the Old Testament, priests, kings, and prophets were anointed. Oil was poured upon the head of the person being anointed (Exodus 29:7) as he was set apart as God's chosen one to do a special work or to stand in a special office.

In the New Testament, the anointing is not just for priests, kings, and prophets. It is for all who believe in the Lord Jesus Christ. All who are a part of the body of Christ are called God's anointed. We are sealed and set apart for Him (2 Corinthians 1:21-22).

When we receive Jesus Christ as our Lord and Savior, the Holy Spirit comes into our heart (Galatians 4:6). We enter into covenant with God (Hebrew 8:6, 10) and become new creatures in Christ Jesus. Old things are passed away. All things become new (2 Corinthians 5:17). We are born again and have eternal life (John 3:3-5, 15–16).

As our relationship with Christ deepens, the Holy Spirit comes upon us to impart supernatural ability (Acts 1:8). We are empowered to prosper, to walk in health and our divine destiny. We are equipped for service.

It is not just a physical anointing, but a spiritual anointing as well; it is the Holy Spirit touching our hearts and minds with God's love and truth.

As the anointing manifests itself in our lives, the Holy Spirit molds us and shapes us into the vessels He intends us to be (Philippians 1:6). He is the Potter, and we are the clay. When we seek Him with all of our heart, thus begins a breaking process as He twists and pulls, tugs and turns our clay into a form that He can sculpt (Isaiah 64:8).

In this book, I especially speak to women.

There is neither male nor female in Christ Jesus (Galatians 3:28). We are all one in Him, having been baptized into the Body of Christ by the Holy Spirit (1 Corinthians 12:12-13). However, women have been the target of the enemy since the beginning (Genesis 3:1-15). Worldwide, we have been oppressed, rejected, and dismissed as inferior and of little value.

This is a lie and must be addressed. Jesus Christ is our Redeemer (Colossians 1:13–14). There is no way to be free but in Him (John

8:31–32, 36). Women, no matter our race, creed, or culture, are set free by His resurrecting power (John 11:25). The anointing is this power to achieve our hopes and dreams and to walk in our purpose; it is a gift from God.

We are made in God's image (Genesis 1:26–27). There are no two people alike. Even identical twins have one or two distinguishing characteristics that separate one from the other.

As we walk in our covenant rights, we no longer think the same, act the same, or look the same. We begin to look holy and righteous, taking on the very nature of God. The Spirit of the Lord begins to rise up within us, and we begin to desire for ourselves what the Father desires—the best, the absolute best.

No one loves you more than the Father does. He sent His Son to die for you (John 3:16). How can we think of ourselves as small when such a great God loves us? We are the apple of His eye

(Deuteronomy 32:10), and as such, we should feel special indeed. We should discover our purpose, the reason we were born, what we are here for, and what God intended us to be. God has an expected end for us (Jeremiah 29:11). As we spend time in His Word and His Presence, we desire all that He has for us, and we rise to the mountaintop to be all that we are ordained to be.

This anointing is for every believer. It is to help you find your destiny and walk with purpose, leaving nothing behind and losing no opportunity. It is to direct you to your right path in life so that you will have no regrets. It is God's power to ascend to the mountaintop.

We have been given all authority and dominion to reign on the earth in victory (Matthew 28:18–20). God expects us to do this. God expects us to increase (Psalm 115:14). He expects us to possess our land (Deuteronomy 6:18). He came that we might have life and live life more abundantly (John 10:10). He wants to enlarge us (1

Chronicles 4:10) and take us from glory to glory (2 Corinthians 3:18). He places His desire in our heart. As we meditate on His Word and allow His Holy Spirit to develop our imagination and creative ability, what was once a hope becomes a reality. What was once a dream becomes a fervent expectation as we continue to meditate on those things that we desire (Joshua 1:8).

Jesus set us free from the law of sin and death (Romans 8:2). He gave us the victory over all principalities and powers, triumphing over them openly (Colossians 2:15). We have authority to walk in all our covenant rights, and He expects us to do so. Anything else is a travesty, for He lay down His glory to descend to earth to show us how to live this life (John 17:5).

As we walk in our authority, we experience victory over sickness, fear, poverty, lack, depression, addiction, low self-esteem, and all things that are not of God. When we come into the understanding of who we are in Him, we think differently and act differently.

We become who we think we are (Proverbs 23:7). We expect the best, and more importantly, we demand it of everything in our lives. We act royally, and anything not in line with God's plan for our lives becomes a weight that easily besets us (Hebrews 12:1).

All of us were born with a purpose. God knew exactly what He wanted when He spoke us into existence. What He wants for us is His best. When He places His desire in our heart, it forms an image in our spirit that grows until what was once impossible becomes possible.

We see ourselves as God sees us: as royalty. The anointing that abides within us is an anointing of ascension. Once it manifests, it will take the believer who walks by faith to the mountaintop.

We have victory over everything that is not of God. If something is not like Him, we sidestep around it and keep moving forward. As we follow our heart and nurture and develop our gifts and talents, the anointing brings people, opportunities, and experiences our way to keep us on the path that we should follow. As we walk on this road, who we are and what we are becomes crystal clear to us. Our vision becomes a sharper image until there is no denying it. This is God's desire for us—to see what He sees and to walk in it. The anointing is the power of God to push and catapult you into fulfilling His purpose.

How do you walk in this anointing? By having faith in God and believing that He has a plan for your life; by asking Him to direct and guide you, and keep you from taking a wrong turn; by continual prayer and supplication to God, thanking Him and praising Him for what He is doing in your life; by obedience to His Word; and by living a life of holiness. But most of all, you walk in His anointing by worshipping Him.

Worship is exalting God for who He is. As we worship God because He is great and mighty, a wonderful Counselor, the Prince of Peace, the great I Am, the King of kings and the Lord of lords, God's glory descends upon us because He seeks those who will worship Him (John 4:23). When we bask in His glory continually, all that He has for us becomes possible.

When we enter into praise and worship, the image of who we are becomes clearer to us. There grows within us such a fervent expectation of what we desire to manifest that we make a violent demand on our covenant to produce kingdom living. This is scriptural; as the Bible says in Matthew 11:12, the violent take the kingdom of God by force.

We command the circumstances in our lives to change. We call those things that be not as though they were (Romans 4:17); we expect change and transformation, for we are following the example of God. He said, "Let there be light," and light was (Genesis 1:3). We speak to our situations and expect obstacles to move. If our words are spoken in faith, they will. We believe; therefore, we speak (2 Corinthians 4:13).

Faith is the substance of things hoped for, the evidence of things not seen (Hebrews 11:1). When we walk by faith and not by sight, we see the manifestation of what we have believed unfolding in our lives (2 Corinthians 5:7). When we step out in faith, acting on God's Word to us, we develop a confidence that can't be shaken.

We continually bombard heaven with our thanksgiving and praise, knowing that because God hears us, He will give us what we desire of Him (1 John 5:14–15). He is a covenant-keeping God (Psalms 89:34), and when we keep His commandments and do what is pleasing in His sight, we receive those things for which asked (1 John 3:22).

Even when we miss the mark, God is faithful. His mercies are new every morning and great is His faithfulness (Lamentations 3:22–23). If we confess our sins, He is faithful and just to forgive our sins and to cleanse us from all unrighteousness (1 John 1:9). When we know who we are and understand our covenant, we know that there is nothing that can stop us. No weapon formed against us shall prosper (Isaiah 54:17), and nothing can separate us from the love of God (Romans 8:38–39). We know that we are the apple of His eye (Zechariah 2:8), and He continually perfects those things that concern us (Psalms 138:8).

We don't experience angst over our delays or fret over what we can't see; instead, we just continually trust Him and wait on Him knowing that He is not a man that He should lie (Numbers 23:19), but in His time and season, it will come to pass.

There is a season for everything under heaven (Ecclesiastes 3:1), and God knows the perfect season and the set time for you (Psalms 102:13). He knows when you are mature enough to handle certain things, and when some things would lead to your destruction. We must trust God in all things, knowing that all things work together for good to those who love God and are called according to His purpose (Romans 8:28).

The Anointing of the Queen

The anointing of the queen is the anointing to rule over your life, your circumstances, your surroundings, your community, and the plans of your enemies. It is the anointing of Esther, a woman in obscurity called to the throne for such a time as this (Esther 4:14). It is an anointing from God Almighty to the daughters of Zion to come up higher and to take their rightful place in His kingdom.

No matter where we find ourselves, the goal is to ascend to the next level, line upon line, precept upon precept, here a little, there a little, from glory to glory (Isaiah 28:10; 2 Corinthians 3:18). Even in our lowest state, we can speak the Word of God in our lives to effect change.

The anointing of the queen is an anointing of ascension. It is one of recognition and acceptance of who you are. It is one of embracing your greatness and knowing that when you look in the mirror, a queen looks back. It is one of self-confidence and expectancy, but also of humility and grace. It is one of strength yet softness, of maturity yet innocence, of willfulness yet yieldedness. It is the anointing of the woman, the wife, the mother, the daughter, the sister. It is the female gender in her highest state: the state created by God for Eve that was lost in the Garden of Eden because of her disobedience (Genesis 3:1–24).

Has it been redeemed? Yes, on the cross by Jesus Christ. All that was lost to us as women was redeemed by His death, burial, and resurrection. All that the enemy stole was given back to us as

Christ Himself ascended to His throne to take His rightful place as Lord of all (Mark 16:19).

We are His workmanship (Ephesians 2:10), and as such, we are cloaked in His glory (John 17:22). When we speak, we frame our world (Hebrews 11:3). When we look in the mirror and see royalty, we speak into the atmosphere and create change.

The anointing of the queen is on every Christian woman who walks in all that God has given her.

How does she do this? She understands who she is: the redeemed of the Lord, and the daughter of the Most High. She sees herself in the Word. She calls those things that be not as though they were (Romans 4:17). She spends time with God. She spends time with those around her, for she is diligent to be who she is: one who helps and blesses others because she lives the Word in her daily life.

How do you become this woman? It is a continual process of being purified in the fire of the Holy Ghost (Malachi 3:2–3). As you walk with God and fellowship with Him, you will want what He wants, which is always the best for you. In all things, expect the best as you walk with purpose.

What is the best? Does it not depend on who you are, where you are, and your particular circumstances? Cannot the best for the homemaker be a happy home, a satisfied husband, well-raised children, time for herself, and quality time with her family? For the career woman, can it not be the promotion to the highest level of her career without deceit or guile, allowing God to do a work in her as she ascends? For the woman in ministry, can it not be the continual growth of a ministry according to God's Word as she walks in maturity and grace? For the teenager in school, can it not be getting the best grades while working toward a goal God has placed in her heart?

For all women, can it not be following the desires of your heart, that small nudge in your spirit that won't go away? What would you do if there were no financial restraints, husband, or children in your life? Can you not still do it? Will your family not be an added blessing to share in your success? You can be a dancer, a singer, a teacher, and a doctor. You can be a business-woman, a mogul, or an entrepreneur. You can be and do all things in Christ Jesus who strengthens you, for this is His desire (Philippians 4:13).

Expect no less than the best. Do not be denied by others' opinions of you or their low expectations. God expects you to ascend, to come up higher (Revelation 4:1), to see through His eyes, and to walk in your anointing.

Oh, Queen, who has called you less than who you are? Sidestep and regroup but keep ascending. When derailed, get up, shake yourself off, and continue to ascend. Never stop. Never regress. Always ascend. Always strive toward your goal, for what queen is denied? Who can stop her but the king? Our King has extended His scepter toward us (Esther 5:2). The kingdom is ours to possess. We are to possess our land (Leviticus 20:24).

How do you walk in this anointing? How do you develop the mentality of a queen? Think the best. Choose the best. Desire the best. Watch and see what happens as you experience another level. As you begin to experience the best, you will want only the best in all areas. If you are not walking with purpose, you will quickly become dissatisfied.

Start where you are. You can walk in this anointing no matter your age, race, or nationality. Aspire to greatness. See the cup of your life as full to overflowing. Identify your gifts and hone them. If you like to sing, then sing. Learn music and write songs. Whatever your heart's desire, it is God tugging on your heart and saying, "Come this way. Come up to a higher place."

Hear His voice as He calls you into destiny. Hear His voice as He calls you into purpose. Do not allow the fear of the unknown to keep you from striving toward your desire. Walk by faith and not by sight (2 Corinthians 5:7). See the end before you begin. Call those things that be not as though they were (Romans 4:17). Always expect to walk in what you believe. It will surely happen if you hold fast to your profession of faith (Hebrews 10:23).

What are you professing? What do you believe? What do you believe that you can do, be, and accomplish? See yourself as you desire to be. See yourself as a doctor, even if you are sitting in a biology class. See yourself as a scientist, even if you are sitting in the back of a bus with no money. See yourself as a homeowner, even if you are lying on a cot in a homeless shelter.

If you can see it, you can believe it. When you believe it, you will speak it. As you speak it, you will expect it (2 Corinthians 4:13). As you expect it, you will see the manifestation of what you believe (Mark 11:23–24). We are to be like God. Just as He spoke this world into existence, we can speak our worlds into existence (Genesis 1:1-31). When we walk as He walked, we will walk in the glory of God.

Allow no one to keep you from walking in destiny. Many will look at you and say, "Who is she to think of herself as a queen?" They will assume that you are being arrogant, but the truth is that you are just self-assured and confident. Is this mindset condescending to others? No. It is simply you walking in your covenant rights—your God-ordained destiny.

❦

The Servant's Heart

Who is a queen? One who is humble and has a contrite spirit; one who is willing to lead yet follow; one who will serve yet teach; one who will give, then receive; one who knows God and His Word.

Have a servant's heart. The greatest in the kingdom is the servant, the one who will sacrifice for others—not just for family members, but for those who God places in her life. If the Good Samaritan could help a stranger (Luke 10:30–37), how much more can a queen walk in God's love? To serve is to honor God, yourself, and your fellow man.

How do you serve? You serve by obeying God and being a doer of His Word and not a hearer only (James 1:23). Take the position that no matter what happens in life, you will honor God. Help the poor, lay hands on the sick, and preach the Gospel to a lost and dying world (Matthew 11:5). You can also clean your neighbor's house when she is sick, babysit your best friend's children when she is feeling overwhelmed, or offer to work late so that a co-worker can leave. This is serving.

To have a servant's heart is to humble yourself, to walk with the dignity and grace of a queen without being arrogant, cocky, or demanding. Command respect by your very presence, yet submit to the authority that has been placed over you.

To have a servant's heart is to serve quietly when others around you are being promoted, even if they have less experience and maturity in their Christian walk. To have a servant's heart is to sing in the background when you can lead the vocals, to take out the trash, clean the toilets, and greet the people when you can preach the sermon. To have a servant's heart is to take a backseat in the church and allow yourself to be exalted in due season; to wait on the Lord to promote you; to let another praise you. The servant's heart is meek, kind, quiet yet strong, never calculating, never cocky, cunning, or duplicitous, and always instant in season, ready to help and serve (2 Timothy 4:2).

A servant loves to give of herself, her time, her money, and her emotions. She is always sympathetic to the poor, and she is generous, resourceful, full of information and compassion, and ready to go the extra mile when asked, never refusing to give when able to do so.

Every queen has a servant's heart. It is impossible to be without it, for the greatest in the kingdom is the servant (Matthew 23:11) who is willing to wash the feet of another while walking in power and love (John 13:3–5).

The apostle is a servant, the prophet is a servant, the teacher is a servant, the evangelist is a servant, and the pastor is a servant.

Do you have to be in the ministry to be a servant? No, but you do need to love God and His people. A woman with a servant's heart will volunteer at a senior citizens' home when her parents are long gone. She will work at a daycare center even though she has no children of her own. She will work with the sick even though she may be ill herself. She will serve food in a soup kitchen when her cupboards are bare. The woman with a servant's heart will sacrifice for strangers when no one sacrifices for her. God's love will be shed abroad in her heart (Romans 5:5). God's love will be seen in her.

The true queen has a servant's heart and wishes no more than to please the Father in all that she does (Colossians 1:10).

Worship and praise define her life (Psalm 34:1). Living to give is a parameter of her existence, for if she is unable to give, she becomes frustrated in the knowledge that she is not walking with purpose (Luke 6:38). The true queen has a heart to give as well as to serve because the two go hand in hand.

When walking in love, power, and strength, she holds her neighbor in high esteem and loves her neighbor as herself (Matthew 22:39). She sees a need and fills it. She sees a hurting soul and offers comfort. She sees the lost and speaks the Word of God to provide direction. She is as Esther, born for such a time as this (Esther 4:14).

How many are true queens? As many as will allow the Holy Spirit to mold and shape them into vessels of honor. Honor is the operative word. Do you honor yourself? Then honor your neighbor, your co-worker, and your family member (Romans 13:7). Do unto others as you would have them do unto you (Luke 6:31). Walk as the Savior walked—in love.

The Power to Love

The love walk requires grace, mercy, humility, and power. The power to love is given by God. It is inherent in the anointing of the queen, because to walk as a queen requires a heart for God's people—a love for humanity.

The ability to see the pain of suffering and mourn its effect in people's lives is a part of the love walk. To be patient, kind, and long-suffering is a part of the love walk (1 Corinthians 13:4). Neither rude nor envious, the queen walks this walk with the joy of the Lord, who is her strength (Nehemiah 8:10). She praises the Lord daily and thanks God for every valley, for she knows it will only strengthen her (1 Thessalonians 5:18). Hers is a testing ground, a proving ground, just as God proved Abraham with Isaac (Genesis 22:1–12).

Even when you are walking in the anointing of the queen, you will be called upon to do things that are not to your liking. How you respond will determine the length of your test, thus perfecting your love walk. Will you endure insults, humiliation, doubt, and fear? Will you continue to stand, and having done all, to still stand (Ephesians 6:13)? Or will you murmur and complain, and shrink into the abyss of indecision, never moving forward, looking back with regret, wondering where you went wrong?

If you truly are a queen, a disciple of Christ, you will not allow fear and doubt to paralyze and inhibit your thoughts and actions. You will love yourself enough to want God's best, and you will speak what you believe and step out in faith.

The power to love is not just an outward expression toward others, but it is also the ability to love oneself: to look in the mirror and be satisfied with who is staring back. The power to love is the ability to see love handles at the waistline and rejoice anyway; to see gray hairs and wrinkles and say, "Hallelujah!" The power to love is to see extra weight in all the wrong places and know that you are loved by a Supreme Being. The power to love is to see a husband walk out, a child die, a best friend leave, or to suffer the loss of a loved one and still sing a song of praise to the Lord.

Love is kind, love endures, love never gives up, love is all things pertaining to God, for God is good and God is love (1 John 4:16).

Love is not puffed up, love does not boast, love does not gossip or slander. Love does not envy or covet. Love does not secretly plot or cause others to stumble. Love waits, love helps, love builds up, love edifies, love strengthens, love tests, love trusts, love walks by faith. Love is God, and God is love (1 Corinthians 13:1–13).

God requires the queen to walk in love, for the love of God is shed abroad in her heart (Romans 5:5). It is agape love, the kind of love that will forgive an enemy and allow you to help those who have hurt you; it is the kind of love that sees someone's bound and conflicted soul underneath the mask of hatred he or she wears.

Love waits on God to lead and guide. The queen who walks in love is powerful indeed, for she has control over her circumstances.

Much is accomplished by choosing to love. Strife is avoided, grudges are nullified, and for-giveness is the order of the day. Marriages are saved, best friends remain, and children return home.

Love allows the queen to rule and reign, for this is her purpose.

To Rule And Reign

*T*hose who possess the anointing of the queen will want to be the best they can be. The highest in all fields will be their aspiration. Even though they may start at the bottom, they are always looking up. They will own the business, not work for it. They are real estate moguls, bankers, and private investors.

The good life beckons to them even when they're unemployed and their situation seems hopeless. To others, they are dreamers who live in a fantasy world, but they know in their heart that theirs is a real dream, a true desire that is achievable if they are consistent and persistent.

A true queen can't be persuaded or dissuaded. She will persist, pursue, and prevail, for she must rule and reign in all of her endeavors. Like cream, she must rise to the top, never stopping until she achieves her goal. If she is sidetracked or derailed, she lifts herself up and starts again like a heat-guided missile ever pursuing her target.

She will not be deterred, for she is determined to be the best that she can be. She is determined to follow her heart.

She is fearless in the pursuit of her dream, asking questions of strangers, receiving information, knowing that those who have not are those who ask not (James 4:2).

She is relentless, like a hungry lioness, finding out what she needs, what to do, where to go, for each step is planned and carefully thought out. She seeks the Lord and walks by faith, but she understands that faith without works is dead

(James 2:26). She prays without ceasing (1 Thessalonians 5:17) and seeks wise counsel. She puts her effort where her faith is and steps out.

She is a woman whose husband can safely trust in her and whose children call her blessed (Proverbs 31:10–31). She runs her household well, and with her earnings, she invests. She has earnings, for the woman who walks in the anointing of the queen is drawn to wealth—not wealth in and of itself, but what financial freedom can provide.

She is seated in heavenly places (Ephesians 2:6). She is more than a conqueror (Romans 8:37). She is the apple of God's eye and is made in His image. She walks erect and statuesque, knowing that all of heaven is in full support of her God-ordained efforts as she walks by faith and not by sight (2 Corinthians 5:7).

Her faith is pleasing to God (Hebrew 11:6) because she is not lukewarm and does not draw back; instead, she is consistent and fully persuaded that she will receive what she has chosen to believe (Romans 4:19–21). Her belief is so strong that circumstances and the storms of life cannot deter her. They only make her stronger. This woman is as strong as a lioness but as meek as a lamb. She is as hard as nails but as soft as silk. She is a living, breathing oxymoron, for she is a daughter, a wife, a servant, a boss, a mother, a sister, a neighbor, and a friend.

She is Deborah, Esther, Sarah, Rachel, Rahab, Miriam, Mary, Elizabeth—the living embodiment of all the women of God, all walking different paths, all chosen by God. She is powerful yet vulnerable, for all who possess a nurturing spirit are vulnerable. To rule and reign requires an inner resolve, a quiet strength, and a fierce determination that she will succeed. Like a lioness protecting her cubs, she will allow nothing and no one to deter her. Once her dream is achieved, nothing or no one will take it away. She will do all she can to possess the land (Deuteronomy 1:8).

The true queen casts her cares upon the Lord (1 Peter 5:7) and enters into His rest (Hebrews 4:3, 9–10). She rests in a dwelling place, a secret place (Psalm 91:1) in fellowship and intimacy with God, knowing that He is well able to keep and preserve all that she has obtained by faith. As she rules and reigns, she also rests.

The Spirit of Royalty

The spirit of royalty is one of achievement. Those who possess the anointing of the queen possess the spirit of royalty.

Women with the anointing of the queen create an oasis in the middle of a desert. Even in dire circumstances, they create a safe haven that seems to their children like heaven on earth.

Those who possess the spirit of royalty walk as a queen no matter their circumstances. It is easy to have the best and reign on the mountaintop when the way is paved for you and money is no problem, but what of the woman who faces barrier after barrier, and whose resources are limited? What does she do? If she possesses a spirit of royalty, she climbs over each barrier one at a time, for she must be who she was born to be.

The woman in the ghetto who desires a college education might have to work three jobs and take as many buses to class, but nothing will deter her. For the single mother who desires a better life for her children, late nights under a study lamp may be her life for several years as she pursues her goal.

For the welfare mom who is told that she can never be anything, acquiring a GED and job training may be her goal as she climbs over the barrier of dependency to freedom from others controlling her life.

For the battered woman, a spirit of royalty will drive her out of a loveless marriage and into a shelter, for she possesses a will to be who she was born to be: a queen made in God's image, not a punching bag for a coward and a bully.

For the abused young girl neglected in foster care, a spirit of royalty will cause her to desire a family of her own, never having to depend on others for the basic necessities of life.

For the soccer mom who has spent years putting her family first, a spirit of royalty will cause her to pursue a hidden desire: running her own business.

For the wife and mother, a spirit of royalty will cause her to run for political office with no experience in order to make a change in her world.

For the illiterate and uneducated woman, a spirit of royalty will drive her to seek an education so that she will no longer live in shame or fear of being discovered.

For every woman, no matter her circumstance, rich or poor, educated or uneducated, married or single, children or no children, the spirit of royalty, inherent in the anointing of the queen, will cause her to strive toward what God has intended her to be.

Make a decision to start toward your goal. The anointing of the queen will carry you forward as you take step after step. Each decision can be a right one or a wrong one. Does it help you obtain your goal? Does this friendship help or hurt you? Are these people in your corner? Are they cheering for you or secretly wishing your downfall?

Trust your spirit. You will know what to do. As you spend time with God in fellowship and worship, you will be directed to the right course of action. You will know what to do in all things (1 John 2:20).

Fellowship With The Father

What is fellowship with the Father? Fellowship with the Father is spending time in His Presence, communing with Him in His Word, singing a song of praise in a secret place, and praying with a pure heart in your prayer closet. Fellowship with the Father is the primary thing that develops your relationship with Him.

Fellowship produces such intimacy with God that you begin to feel invincible. This closeness empowers you to believe and know that you can fail at nothing when you do all things through

Christ Jesus who strengthens you (Philippians 4:13).

Just as David knew he could win against the uncircumcised Philistine (1 Samuel 17:26, 45–46), you will know that you can conquer the "giants" in your life. This oneness with God will produce such confidence that you will run toward what others shrink from. This winner's attitude comes from within as you spend hours in fellowship with the Father.

In His Presence, there is fullness of joy and pleasures evermore (Psalm 16:11). The joy of the Lord is your strength (Nehemiah 8:10), and it is evident in the newfound attitude of one who has been in fellowship with God.

Fellowship with the Father brings a closeness, a oneness, a bond like no other. This produces a queenly anointing, and the ascension to that role in His timing, and when that happens a queen has emerged, and she must be crowned. She must take her rightful place. For we are seated in heavenly places (Ephesians 2:6), and the more time we spend with God, the more we become like Him.

Oneness with God transcends time, space, and energy. It is the key ingredient in the metamorphosis of the ordinary woman into the extraordinary woman who walks in all God has ordained for her. As gifts and talents arise and are unleashed, an even greater fellowship is necessary. It is like the air we breathe—invisible, but oh so necessary.

As we fellowship with the Father, we become more like Him: long-suffering, slow to anger, kind, peaceful, merciful, and generous (Psalm 86:15; 145:8). We love with an unconditional love that surprises others, but most of all ourselves.

It is sometimes difficult for those closest to us to watch this transformation, for others are most comfortable with us in our weaknesses, not our strengths. As the queen in us emerges, it can produce a hostile attitude from those who would choose to see us remain in a cocoon like a cater-pillar, not a butterfly that's broken free of her constraints. Those who prefer to see us as we once were feel threatened at the emergence of the queen in us, transforming us into a woman of honor.

Their comfort level and emotional well-being is shaken as they ponder, *Who is she to act so privileged and favored?* Those without a relationship with God will be highly offended and will either run away or remain and attack our confidence, our emotions, our state of mind, and sometimes our physical bodies.

We must be steadfast in our purpose. We must remain focused and keep our feet firmly planted on our God-ordained path. All God has given to us can be lost if we deviate from what He has placed in our hearts and instructed us to do. As we fellowship with the Father and walk in forgiveness, He will give us the peace that passes all understanding (Philippians 4:6). He will help us to walk in love and obey.

Obedience

As we emerge in all of our glory, we know that behind us is a journey of twists and turns, hilltops and valleys. No one walks a totally straight path. There are disappointments and celebrations. It is challenging and sweet at the same time.

What must we do when we are in the valley waiting for the morning to come? Obey God! What must we do when all the powers of darkness are aligned against us? Obey God! Hear the Word of the Lord and obey. Worship and praise God for what He has done, is doing, and will do. We must obey God when we are aching, crying, hurting, and feeling life's pressures. We must obey Him when those we love hurt and betray us, for obedience is better than sacrifice (1 Samuel 15:22), and it is the road to victory.

How many have missed God's blessing because when they heard His voice, they turned a deaf ear on Him instead of responding to His call? How many have settled for mediocrity when greatness could have been theirs if only they had followed the Word instead of the opinion of man?

Who knows you better than the Father? Who loves you more than God? Who has your life in His hand? A life of obedience to God will lead to a life of blessing (Deuteronomy 28:1–14). There are conditions and prerequisites, but if you follow God's plan, you will walk in all that He has destined for you.

How do you follow God's plan? Follow your heart. In the face of adversity, follow your heart. When all opinions are contrary to yours, follow your heart. Follow your heart no matter what, for the Spirit of Truth is leading you. He is teaching you all things (John 14:17, 26).

Whatever you long for, think about, and yearn to do, do it. Do nothing that makes you feel less than whom you are. You will know what to do by the peace that is in your heart. Let the peace of God rule in your heart (Colossians 3:15), for the peace of God passes all understanding (Philippians 4:7). God's peace will lead you to make right decisions. Right decisions will lead you to a place of blessing.

Do not martyr your dreams, visions, or passions to please others. Please only God, and see Him move supernaturally in your life. See Him do a work in you. See Him crown you Queen.

Ascension

$\mathcal{T}$he anointing of the queen is quite powerful, for once it manifests, mediocrity can no longer be tolerated. The anointing produces a resistance so powerful in its scope that others will perceive your confidence as arrogance. This anointing is obtained by receiving Jesus Christ as your Lord and Savior. It manifests in your life through obedience: by spending time alone with God and fellowshipping with Him. Hours in prayer, studying the Word, and praise and worship will take you to another level in God. You will see yourself as the Father sees you: a child of the King. You will expect favor, provision, healing, and success, all of what belongs to you as a part of your covenant with God.

As you rise to the position of Queen, you will yearn for what God has placed within your heart: greatness.

Greatness requires great faith. It requires a belief in the impossible, the miraculous, and the excessive. What others dream about becomes your norm. What others fantasize about becomes your fervent expectation. You expect favor in every circumstance, and you wonder why it doesn't manifest on the rare occasions when it does not.

As you rise, you will shed the skin of the old you in order to allow your inner beauty to shine through. It is the work of the Lord as He gives you beauty for ashes, and as He chisels you for His glory (Isaiah 61:3).

How does He do this? He allows situations to come into your life that force you to choose this day who you will serve. As you make conscious decisions to side with God, you will ascend (Joshua 24:15).

Will it be easy? No, because every attack of the enemy will come your way to dissuade you and tempt you to give up. All of the forces of darkness will gather against you to keep you distracted, confused, and frustrated in order to accomplish one thing: to keep your eyes off your ultimate destination—the mountaintop. That is where purpose lies, and God will give you a strategy to achieve it. Like Gideon, you will be called a mighty woman of valor long before you achieve victory (Judges 6:12).

How do you remain focused? How do you continue to ascend as you are buffeted on every side by the cares of life? You worship. You praise. You sit in the stillness of God's Presence expecting to hear from Him (Psalm 46:10). You draw close to Him in your intimate moments, so close that His Presence becomes palpable. You enter into the Holy of Holies (Hebrew 10:19-22) and rest in His dwelling place (Psalm 90:1).

You sit still in His glory and allow Him to restore, renew, and refresh your spirit. In other words, you trust God and His Word, for He and His Word are one (John 1:1).

As you rise, know that if God is for you, who can be against you (Romans 8:31)? The God of all the earth has made a righteous decree on your behalf. You are accepted in the beloved (Ephesians 1:6), and you are exalted (James 1:9).

You are exalted for service, exalted to rule and reign, exalted to operate in the gifts of the spirit (1 Corinthians 12:1-11), and to pour out every talent that was birthed in you. This is the desire of the Father's heart: that we take our place as children of the Most High God, for we have been made kings and priests (Revelation 1:6).

Beauty For Ashes

The Word says that God will give us beauty for ashes (Isaiah 61:3). We are lifted up out of the miry clay to be poured into, loved unconditionally, and chiseled into greatness (Psalm 40:2).

As Esther, we are to come to the King purified and prepared (Esther 2:12-13). She was unknown, but because of her beauty, she was brought to the forefront. Is beauty only physical? Can it not be spiritual and emotional? Cannot the anointing of God make beautiful what was once dark and ugly? Will He not give beauty for ashes, the God of glory (Isaiah 61:3)?

Once a dejected woman, the true queen understands that beauty comes from within. True beauty is what is in you: love, joy, peace, and contentment. It radiates upon one's face. A woman of God who understands who she is will radiate an inner glow that will draw others to her like a magnet.

Who is this woman? She is you, and she is me. She will not allow others' opinions of her to define her. What others think of her is of no concern, for she knows that she is the apple of the Father's eye. It is His opinion that counts and His alone.

Words can frame a world (Hebrews 11:3), and what we think becomes who we are (Proverbs 23:7). What others say about you can only affect you if you accept and embrace what is said as true. Reject anything that is not the Word of God. You are fearfully and wonderfully made (Psalm 139:14). Perfect and magnificent, there is no one like you; you are a rare jewel indeed.

Think of yourself as a specialty item, so rare that the Father would send His only begotten Son to save you, to deliver you, and to set you free (John 3:16).

When we see ourselves as God sees us, we see ourselves as one with God (John 17:21). What He has, we have. What He possesses, we possess.

What do you desire? Begin to decree it. Begin to form your world by the words you speak. Agree with God. He says that you can have what you say. He says that when you pray, you are to believe that you have already received what you are praying for and you shall have it (Mark 11:23–24). He says you are His anointed (2 Corinthians 1:21-22). Walk in the anointing and be blessed.

"How great thou art," sings the Psalmist. God is a wonder, He is awesome, He is majestic, He is royalty, and so are we. We who are made in His image, we also are awesome, majestic, and glorious. We are all these things because God's Spirit lives within us. The same Spirit that raised Christ from the dead dwells in our mortal bodies (Romans 8:11). How can we be anything but great?

What do we do with greatness? We use it for mankind. We serve with a hunger and a zeal for God. We honor God with our obedience and love. We love unconditionally those who come across our path and those with whom we are connected.

We strive for excellence (Ecclesiastes 9:10) in all that we do, yet we deflect glory and praise, knowing all too well that our gifts and talents originate from the Father, and the glory is His alone (1 Corinthians 1:29).

In Him, we live and move and have our being (Acts 17:28). Apart from Him, we are nothing. We can't live without Him, nor do we care to. How can we exist in this earthly realm without a Master or Creator? How can we come to God without a Savior (John 14:6)? What a wondrous

God we serve! How we humble ourselves before Him as we recognize His awesome Presence!

"Holy! Holy! Holy!" cry the angels in heaven as they stand in awe of His wonder. "Holy! Holy! Holy!" we cry as we display the same reverence for the King of kings and the Lord of lords.

We are His daughters, and as such, we must walk as He walked, love as He loves, and give as He gives. He is our Master, and we are His disciples. He is our Teacher, our Comforter, our Guide, our everything (John 14:26; 16:13).

We say, "Thank You, Lord, for our salvation." We sing praises to Your name. We glorify Your majesty. We say, "How great is our God!" We say, "I am made in God's image. I am majestic, I am royalty, I am awesome, I am a wonder. I am a queen!

We say, "Thank you, O God!"

www.ingramcontent.com/pod-product-compliance
Lightning Source LLC
Chambersburg PA
CBHW031330040426
42443CB00005B/277